D0768480

Best Easy Day Hikes
North Cascades

Help Us Keep This Guide Up to Date

Every effort has been made by the author and editors to make this guide as accurate and useful as possible. However, many things can change after a guide is published—trails are rerouted, regulations change, facilities come under new management, etc.

We would love to hear from you concerning your experiences with this guide and how you feel it could be improved and kept up to date. While we may not be able to respond to all comments and suggestions, we'll take them to heart and we'll also make certain to share them with the author. Please send your comments and suggestions to the following address:

> The Globe Pequot Press
> Reader Response/Editorial Department
> P.O. Box 480
> Guilford, CT 06437

Or you may e-mail us at:

> editorial@GlobePequot.com

Thanks for your input, and happy trails!

Best Easy Day Hikes Series

Best Easy Day Hikes
North Cascades

Second Edition

Erik Molvar

FALCONGUIDES®

GUILFORD, CONNECTICUT
HELENA, MONTANA
AN IMPRINT OF THE GLOBE PEQUOT PRESS

FALCONGUIDES®

Copyright © 2009 by Morris Book Publishing, LLC
A previous edition was published by Falcon Publishing, Inc. in 1998.

Project Manager: Jessica Haberman
Layout: Kevin Mak
Maps © Morris Book Publishing, LLC

Library of Congress Cataloging-in-Publication Data
Molvar, Erik.
  Best easy day hikes North Cascades / Erik Molvar. – 2nd ed.
    p. cm.
  ISBN 978-0-7627-4122-9
  1. Hiking–North Cascades (B.C. and Wash.)–Guidebooks. 2. Hiking–Washington (State)–Guidebooks. 3. North Cascades (B.C. and Wash.)–Guidebooks. 4. Washington (State)–Guidebooks. I. Title.
GV199.42.C37M65 2009
917.97'50443–dc22

2008046126

Printed in the United States of America

10 9 8 7 6 5 4 3 2 1

Contents

Harts Pass and the Pasayten Wilderness

Lake Chelan and the Stehekin Valley

Map Legend

══90══	Interstate Highway
═30═	U.S. Highway
══20══	State Highway
═41═	Local/Forest Roads
= = = =	Unimproved Road
- - - - - - -	Trail
━━━━━	Featured Route
──────	River/Creek
	Glacier
	Wilderness/National Recreation Area
	National Forest/National Park
⁀	Bridge
▲	Campground
▣	Campground (Fires Prohibited)
▲	Campground—Automobile
•—•	Gate
▲	Horse Camp (Fires Allowed)
▲	Horse Camp (Fires Prohibited)
❷	Information
℗	Parking
)(	Pass
▲	Peak
⚠	Pacific Crest Trail
⊞	Picnic Area
■	Point of Interest/Other Trailhead
🛈	Ranger Station
❻	Trailhead
≋	Waterfall
◈	Viewpoint

Acknowledgments

Thanks to Kelly Bush, Hugh Dougher, Marshall Plumer, and other rangers of North Cascades National Park and Okanogan National Forest for providing information and reviewing this book. Rosemary Siefrit and Todd Johnson provided information for the revision. The introductory material is largely the work of Bill Schneider. Special thanks to my wife, Melanie, for providing good company during the field research.

Introduction

What's a "best easy" hike?

Our national parks and forests serve as windows to the natural world, reservoirs of natural beauty and grandeur, and wellsprings of inspiration. As such, they are magnets to people who seek to reestablish their ties with nature, learn more about the world in which we live, or simply find a quiet escape from the hustle and bustle of modern society. The North Cascades feature mountain fastnesses clad in glaciers, azure lakes, and sparkling waterfalls, inviting the visitor to step into the natural world.

Anyone who travels widely in these areas will soon notice that there are two distinct categories of visitors—those who want to immerse themselves in the wilderness of the North Cascades for several days at a time, and those who only have a day or two and would like a choice sampling of the special features of the area. This book is for the second group.

The materials for this guide were gathered as I researched the much larger and more comprehensive book *Hiking the North Cascades*. The larger book covers every trail in the park and the surrounding wilderness areas, including those that are neither best nor easy. *Best Easy Day Hikes* includes only short, less strenuous hikes that showcase the best features of the North Cascades.

These hikes vary in length, but most are short (fewer than 5 miles). Most lack big hills, and those few long grades that appear in this book are tackled in a leisurely fashion. All hikes are on easy-to-follow trails with no off-trail route-finding challenges. Trailhead access is easy for all hikes, and you can reach any of these trailheads with a low-clearance passenger car.

For those of you who have grown accustomed to enjoying day hiking on public lands, the Forest Service has provided a nasty surprise. The Northwest Forest Pass (or a one-day equivalent) must be purchased to access most trailheads on national forest lands in the North Cascades. North Cascades National Park, on the other hand, continues to set a fine example of providing access to excellently maintained day-hiking trails without charging a fee.

Some of the hikes in this book might not seem easy to some but will be easy for others. To help you decide, I've ranked the hikes from easiest to hardest. Please keep in mind that long does not always equal difficult. Other factors, such as elevation gain and trail conditions, have to be considered.

I hope you thoroughly enjoy your "best easy" hiking through the natural wonders of the North Cascades.

Ranking the Hikes

The following list ranks the hikes in this book from easiest to hardest.

Easiest

More Challenging

Zero Impact

Traveling in an area such as the North Cascades is like visiting a famous museum. You obviously don't want to leave your mark on an art treasure in the museum. If everybody who visited the museum left one tiny mark, the piece of art would be destroyed—and what would a big building full of trashed art be worth? The same goes for pristine wilderness like that found in the North Cascades. If we all left just one little mark on the landscape, the wilderness would soon be despoiled.

A wilderness can accommodate plenty of human use as long as everybody treats it with respect. But a few thoughtless or uninformed visitors can ruin it for everyone who follows. And the need for good manners applies to all wilderness visitors, not just backpackers. Day hikers should also adhere strictly to the "zero impact" principles.

Three FalconGuides Principles of Zero Impact

- Leave with everything you brought with you.
- Leave no sign of your visit.
- Leave the landscape as you found it.

Most of us know better than to litter—in or out of the wilderness. Even the tiniest scrap of paper left along the trail or at the campsite detracts from the pristine character of the North Cascades landscape. This means that you should pack out everything, even biodegradable items like orange peels, which can take years to decompose. It's also a good idea to pick up any trash that less considerate hikers have left behind.

To avoid damaging the trailside soil and plants, stay on the main path. Avoid cutting switchbacks and venturing onto fragile vegetation. When taking a rest stop, select a durable surface like a bare log, a rock, or a sandy beach.

Don't pick up "souvenirs" such as rocks, antlers, feathers, or wildflowers. The next person wants to discover them, too, and taking such souvenirs violates park regulations.

Avoid making loud noises that disturb the silence others may be enjoying. Remember, sound travels easily in the outdoors. Be courteous.

When nature calls, use established outhouse facilities whenever possible. If these are unavailable, bury human waste 6 to 8 inches deep and pack out used toilet paper. This is a good reason to carry a lightweight trowel. Keep wastes at least 300 feet away from any surface water or boggy spots.

Finally, and perhaps most importantly, strictly follow the pack-it-in/pack-it-out rule. If you carry something into the wilderness, consume it completely or carry it out with you.

Practice zero impact principles—put your ear to the ground in the wilderness and listen carefully. Thousands of people coming behind you are thanking you for your courtesy and good sense.

Be Prepared

Although the climate of the North Cascades is quite temperate, hikers should prepare themselves for wet or chilly weather by carrying appropriate clothing and equipment. Always bring along rain gear, as rain is a common occurrence in the Pacific Northwest year-round. The weather can also turn cold at any time, particularly along the coastline and at the timberline. Wise hikers dress in layers, with a thick wool sweater or synthetic pile garment to provide insulation. Also remember that even crystalline mountain streams are not safe water sources without treatment; carry plenty of drinking water with you or bring a portable filter to supply your water needs.

The Western Approaches

The broad green waters of the Skagit River, coursing down through a fertile valley from thousands of snowfields and a hundred glaciers, were the original thoroughfare into the North Cascades. Trails used by the Skagit tribe became the packhorse routes of the prospectors and later a railway to support the building of hydroelectric dams on the Skagit during the 1920s. Today, modern visitors follow the asphalt ribbon of Washington Highway 20, which finally breached the mountain fastness in 1972. The Skagit Valley is a broad and lush basin, fed by the abundant rains of Puget Sound, filled with fruit orchards and dairy farms, and bordered by the broad clear-cuts scythed from the forests by an aggressive timber industry. The peripheral ranges of the North Cascades surround the valley, and a multitude of short trails lead to the mountaintops.

The climate here is distinctly maritime; fogs and rainstorms are the defining elements of the landscape. Abundant moisture creates ideal growing conditions for conifers like hemlock and cedar, which attain mighty proportions in the isolated pockets that were never logged off. Especially impressive stands occur at Rockport State Park and along the upper reaches of the Baker River Highway. Above the timberline are lush meadows guarded by peaks where the snowfields linger year-round.

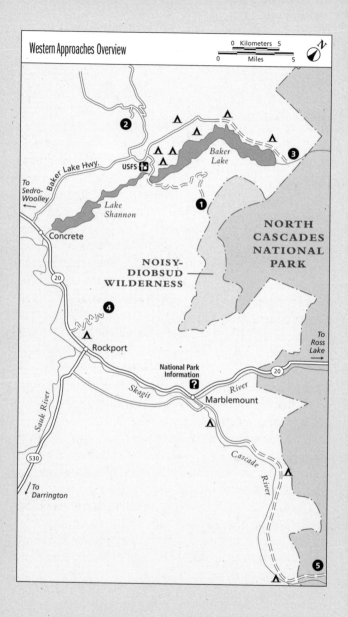

Western Approaches Overview

Because the Skagit Valley is close to both Seattle and Vancouver, British Columbia, it receives quite a bit of weekend tourism. Many of the visitors never venture far from their cars, and the short hikes in the surrounding mountains are well-suited to the tight schedules of a whirlwind tour. Seek out the Park Service ranger station at Marblemount, which is the information center for day hikes and backcountry excursions in the North Cascades National Park complex. Interpretive displays and presentations can be found at the large visitor center just west of Newhalem. Visitors approaching from the west can also obtain information at the joint Forest Service-Park Service station at Sedro-Woolley. The towns of Burlington and Mount Vernon provide all the services of a modern city, while a more limited selection of supplies can be found in Concrete and Marblemount. Rockport has gas and a country store, while Newhalem is a company town built by Seattle City Light for its dam workers and has only a small mercantile concern.

Car campers will find public camping at Rockport State Park as well as the large Park Service campgrounds outside Newhalem. There are a number of Forest Service campgrounds along the Baker River Highway, a paved thoroughfare that originates west of Concrete and follows the shore of Baker Lake, and along the Cascade River Road, a gravel trunk route that runs southeast from Marblemount. User fees are now in effect for all trailheads that fall within the Mount Baker–Snoqualmie National Forest, and apply to day hikers and backpackers alike.

1 Watson Lakes

Type of hike: Out-and-back.
Distance: 7.6 miles.
Time required: 4 to 7 hours.
Elevation change: 780-foot gain.
Best season: Mid-June to mid-October.

Maps: USGS Bacon Peak; Green Trails Lake Shannon.
Jurisdiction: Noisy-Diobsud Wilderness (Mount Baker–Snoqualmie National Forest).

Finding the trailhead: Follow Washington Highway 20 west from Concrete for 5 miles to the Baker River Highway (Forest Road 11). Follow this road north for 14 miles, then turn right at signs for Baker Dam. Drive across the dam and then turn north (left) onto Forest Road 1107, a logging road passable to passenger cars. Follow this road upward for 9.2 miles to a junction with Forest Road 1107-022. Turn left onto this spur and follow it for 1.2 miles to the trailhead.

The Hike

A network of short trails climbs to the timberline at the edge of the Noisy-Diobsud Wilderness, visiting alpine lakes and an old lookout site. Wildflower displays are impressive here, and black bears are commonly sighted. Watson Lakes makes the easiest and most scenic destination, while more ambitious hikers can also opt to visit Anderson Lakes and/or Anderson Butte for a more challenging trip.

The trail begins by ascending gradually across steep slopes robed in an old-growth coastal forest. Western hemlock is the dominant conifer here, but silver fir is also present. Observe the open nature of the forest and the rich mixture of tree sizes: This complexity provides a multitude of ecological niches for forest animals, accounting for the

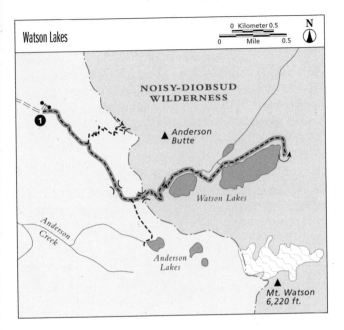

0   Kilometer 0.5

N

0   Mile   0.5

NOISY-DIOBSUD
WILDERNESS

▲ Anderson
Butte

Watson Lakes

Anderson
Creek

Anderson
Lakes

▲ Mt. Watson
6,220 ft.

importance of old growth to forest ecosystems.

After crossing sinuous finger ridges and low saddles, the path emerges unexpectedly into a luxuriant meadow of heather and sedges. The Anderson Butte Trail splits away at the bottom of the meadow, while the main path ascends through the opening to reveal striking views of Mounts Baker and Shuksan to the northwest. Meadows such as these occur in pockets that fill with deep snow, making for a short growing season that effectively excludes most conifers. A few clumps of mountain hemlock grow from the hillocks where the snow melts sooner. Wildlife enthusiasts can glass for pikas in the talus of the lower slopes of Anderson Butte. At the upper edge of the meadow, the trail crosses a pass and enters heavy timber once more. A faint spur path runs to an outcrop that faces southwest for views across Baker Lake.

The main trail descends through the trees to reach a boggy meadow, where the path to Anderson Lakes splits away to the right. The Watson Lakes Trail now climbs vigorously to reach a low notch, then descends into the Noisy-Diobsud Wilderness. Just beyond the boundary, open slopes face eastward across the Watson Lakes for views of majestic Bacon Peak. Hagan Mountain is visible farther to the north. The path now descends sharply to reach camping spots in the heavy timber on the north shore of the western lake.

Our route continues around the lakeshore and crosses the logs at its outlet to reach camping spots amid the heather-sedge parks above the second lake (campers must pitch their tents in designated spots). This lake is the larger of the two, with rocky peninsulas that jut out into the water. The track becomes more primitive as it crosses the log boom at the outlet of the lake and climbs and falls sharply across the hummocky heather. There are excellent views of Martin Peak along the way, and Anderson Butte is unveiled in its rocky majesty from the trail's end on the eastern shore. Turn around here and retrace the trail to complete the hike.

Miles and Directions

- **0.0** Watson Lakes Trailhead
- **0.8** Junction with Anderson Butte Trail (0.7 mile, moderately strenuous). Stay right for Watson Lakes.
- **1.6** Junction with Anderson Lakes Trail (0.9 mile, moderate). Stay left for Watson Lakes.
- **1.9** Trail crosses pass and enters Noisy-Diobsud Wilderness.

2.5	Camping area beside western Watson Lake. Trail follows lakeshore.
2.9	Trail reaches foot of lake.
3.1	Foot of eastern Watson Lake. Trail follows lakeshore.
3.8	Head of eastern Watson Lake. Turn around.
7.6	Arrive back at Watson Lakes Trailhead.

2 Dock Butte–Blue Lake

Type of hike: Out-and-back.
Distance: 4.0 miles.
Time required: All day.
Elevation change: 1,309 foot gain.

Best season: June through September.
Topo Map: Baker Pass.
Jurisdiction: Mount Baker–Snoqualmie National Forest.

Finding the trailhead: Follow Washington Highway 20 west from Concrete for 5 miles to the Baker River Highway (Forest Road 11) at mile 82.5. Follow this paved road north for 8 miles, then turn left on Forest Road 12 just after entering the national forest. Follow this broad gravel road for 7 miles, then turn left on Forest Road 1230. After 4 miles of narrow, winding road, you will reach the trailhead at its end.

The Hike

This short but vigorous day hike climbs to the summit of a small knob that commands views of the Skagit Valley and Mount Baker. A spur trail down to Blue Lake makes an easier destination and is discussed at the end of this section.

The hike begins in subalpine parklands, where mountain hemlocks rise in clusters between heather-filled glades.

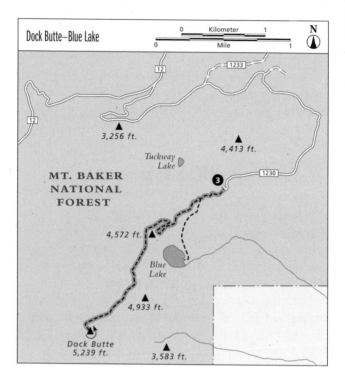

These glades indicate locations where persistent snowdrifts linger into early summer, resulting in a growing season that is too brief to support the establishment of trees. The path runs west and then south across the mountainsides, navigating between the summits of wooded knobs, and soon reaches a pass where the trail splits. To the left is the trail to Blue Lake (see below), while the path to the right begins the hearty climb to the top of Dock Butte.

This trail climbs briskly through the trees, yielding glimpses of Blue Lake and the waterfall that feeds into it. On the north slope of the next knob, a clearing with the first vistas of Mount Baker heralds the approach of the first false summit. The path continues upward, rounding onto west-facing slopes as the trees open up into subalpine parkland.

After you dip to cross a saddle, a calf-burning climb tackles the next summit along the ridgeline. Look north-ward as you ascend: There are superb views to be had of Mounts Baker and Shuksan, with the Twin Sisters rising to the west. Again the path swings onto the western flank of the ridge, and now the sharp prow of Dock Butte can be seen ahead. The path soon begins to ascend the third major pitch, then swings across the north slope of the butte, almost meeting the ridgeline to the west of the summit. It then traverses back across the north slope to meet the spine of the ridge to the east of the summit, and from here it climbs the ridgetop to reach the top of Dock Butte.

Atop Dock Butte, a former fire lookout site presides over a panorama that includes the jagged peaks of North Cascades National Park to the east, with Lake Shannon and Baker Lake laid out in the emerald folds of the foreground. To the south is the Skagit Valley, where the ravages of clear-cutting have left behind a fragmented forest robbed of much of its ecological wealth. Glacier Peak is the nearest of the lofty snowcapped summits that rise beyond the val-ley. To the west, the glittering waters of Puget Sound are framed by the distant Olympic Mountains.

Blue Lake Option. From the junction, the lakebound path makes a level traverse through open woodlands, then climbs steadily across slopes forested with tall hemlocks. It soon reaches a hillock above Blue Lake, which is tucked in a small cirque carved out by a montane glacier, with a slender veil of a waterfall dropping across the cliff that guards its head. It's an easy jaunt from here down through the trees to reach the foot of the lake. The elevation change is 70 feet and the hike is 1.6 miles round-trip.

Miles and Directions

- **0.0** Dock Butte Trailhead.
- **0.2** Trail reaches junction in small saddle. Bear right for Dock Butte; turn left for Blue Lake (0.6 mile farther).
- **2.0** Trail reaches summit of Dock Butte. Turn around.
- **4.0** Arrive back at Dock Butte Trailhead.

3 Baker River

Type of hike: Out-and-back.
Distance: 5.2 miles.
Time required: 2.5 to 4 hours.
Elevation change: 190-foot gain.
Best season: Mid-April to early November.

Maps: USGS Mount Shuksan; Green Trails Mount Shuksan.
Jurisdiction: Mount Baker-Snoqualmie National Forest, North Cascades National Park.

Finding the trailhead: Follow Washington Highway 20 west from Concrete for 5 miles to the Baker River Highway (Forest Road 11). Follow this road north (right). The pavement ends after 20 miles, and at mile 25 there is an unmarked intersection. Turn left for the final mile to the trailhead.

The Hike

This trail penetrates a remote and forgotten corner of North Cascades National Park, offering an easy stroll through the ancient forests along one of the wildest of the Cascades rivers. The trail begins as an old road that wanders

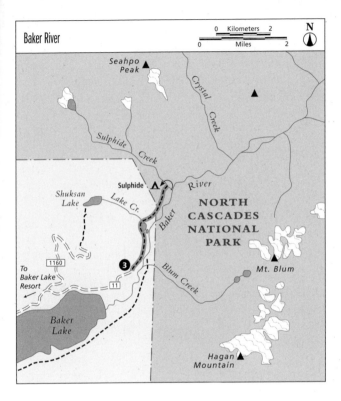

along the riverbanks, which are robed in a young forest of hemlock, cedar, and red alder. Plentiful rainfall creates favorable growing conditions for club moss, which hangs like a shroud from the branches of the vine maples. Soon there are views of the water. The Baker River is young in the geological sense of the word. As it brawls down its steep and gravel-choked course, it splits into broad channels where floodwaters have built up new gravel bars and forced the water to seek a lower passageway. Watch for the glacier-shrouded fastness of Hagan Mountain, which peeks out above the steep foothills beyond the river.

As steep slopes crowd the riverbank, the trail threads its way among massive boulders covered with moss, and ancient cedars tower overhead. The gravel bars farther upstream have been colonized by groves of red alder, which invades flood-scoured riverbanks. Symbiotic bacteria in alder roots pump nitrogen into the soil, where it can nourish the seedlings of the shade-tolerant conifers that ultimately will replace the alders. The trail soon splashes across several tributary streams. The largest of these is Lake Creek, and its alluvial fan supports a fine mixed forest of enormous cedars and moss-draped bigleaf maples.

After a final visit to the river's edge, the path turns inland to bypass an extensive wetland created by beavers. This is an excellent spot to glass for waterfowl and other marsh inhabitants. Returning to the bottomlands, the trail leads onward across the shady floor of a closed-canopy hemlock forest. The understory is suffused with green: Spikemoss grows from every available surface. The trail reaches its end at a Park Service camp beside Sulphide Creek (backcountry permit required). Visit the banks of this brawling stream for northward views of Seahpo Peak at the end of Jagged Ridge. Turn around here and retrace the trail to complete the hike.

Miles and Directions

- **0.0** Trailhead at end of road.
- **1.5** Trail crosses Lake Creek.
- **1.9** Trail enters North Cascades National Park.
- **2.6** Sulphide Camp. Turn around.
- **5.2** Arrive back at the trailhead.

4 Sauk Mountain

Type of hike: Out-and-back.
Distance: 4.2 miles.
Time required: 2 to 3.5 hours.
Elevation change: 1,040-foot gain.
Best season: Mid-May to mid-October.
Maps: USGS Sauk Mountain; Green Trails Lake Shannon.
Jurisdiction: Mount Baker–Snoqualmie National Forest.

Finding the trailhead: Follow Washington Highway 20 to Rockport State Park, just west of Rockport. Drive north on Sauk Mountain Road, an improved gravel road that winds upward for 8 miles to reach the trailhead.

The Hike

This trail makes a short but vigorous ascent to the summit of Sauk Mountain on the seaward edge of the North Cascades. Views are surprisingly inspiring from here, encompassing Mount Baker and Puget Sound as well as the glacier-carved peaks of the Cascades. A spur trail makes a long descent from the heights of Sauk Mountain to reach Sauk Lake, where there are several camping spots. Hikers who are in good physical shape can visit both the summit of Sauk Mountain and Sauk Lake in a hard half-day of hiking.

The trail begins at the timberline, and zigzags steadily up a wide but steep couloir. Avalanches have swept away the trees here, clearing a space for a magnificent display of alpine wildflowers. Glacier and avalanche lilies dominate the early season just after snowmelt and are overtopped by lupine, paintbrush, monkeyflower, penstemon, and many others as the summer progresses. From the slopes, one can look out

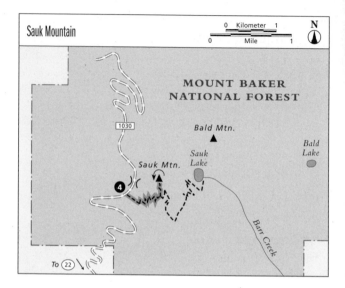

MOUNT BAKER
NATIONAL FOREST

1030

Bald Mtn.

Sauk
Lake

Bald
Lake

Sauk Mtn.

4

Barr Creek

To 22

across the Skagit and Sauk River valleys, with the lofty summit of Whitehorse Mountain rising to the southwest. The icebound volcanic cone of Mount Baker becomes visible near the top of the grade.

The path tops out in a grassy saddle in the rocky cockscomb of Sauk Mountain. Splendid westward views stretch from the high volcanic summit of Glacier Peak north along the western scarp of the Cascade Mountains and into Canada. Strange tors of basalt rise along the crest of Sauk Mountain itself, and small trails wander among them. The main trail traverses high across the eastern face of the peak, and soon the steep spur trail to Sauk Lake drops away to the right. The Sauk Mountain route glides up to a bald knob that offers superb northward views of Mount Shuksan.

The path then crosses the talus slopes beneath a series of sharp pinnacles. Watch for tiny pikas scurrying among the broken shards of rock. The path soon climbs into a saddle and then ascends to the top of one of the pinnacles, where it reaches its end. There is an unobstructed vista of Mount Baker from this point, and on an exceptionally clear day one can see the Olympic Mountains to the west and Mount Rainier to the south. From here, turn around and follow the trail back down to the trailhead.

Miles and Directions

0.0 Sauk Mountain Trailhead.

1.4 Trail reaches ridge crest.

1.6 Junction with spur trail to Sauk Lake (1.5 miles, moderately strenuous). Bear left for summit of Sauk Mountain.

2.1 Trail ends atop one of the crags of Sauk Mountain. Turn around.

4.2 Arrive back at Sauk Mountain Trailhead.

5 Cascade Pass

Type of hike: Out-and-back.
Distance: 7.4 miles.
Time required: 4 to 7 hours.
Elevation change: 1,740-foot gain.
Best season: Mid-July to mid-October.

Maps: USGS Cascade Pass, USGS Goode Mountain; Green Trails Cascade Pass, Green Trails McGregor Mountain.
Jurisdiction: North Cascades National Park.

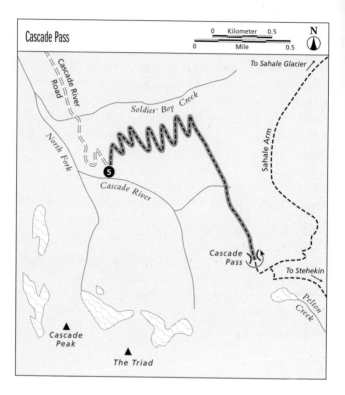

Finding the trailhead: From Marblemount, follow Cascade River Road across the bridge to the trailhead at its end (about 22 miles). The last several miles may be rough with potholes.

The Hike

Perhaps the best-loved trail in the North Cascades, this path has a long climb for an easy hike, but the trail gradient is modest and the trek is suitable even for small children and elderly hikers who are in good health. It follows the ancient trade route used by the Skagit and Chelan peoples to cross the lofty peaks of the divide. Alexander Ross is thought to have bumbled through Cascade Pass during his 1814 explorations on behalf of the Hudson Bay Company. Today, a rugged road leads to the upper basin of the Cascade River's North Fork, from which a moderate trail climbs through the pass and to the headwaters of the Stehekin River. This hike is best saved for weekdays; the parking lot is often overflowing with visitors on the weekends.

The trek begins in the upper basin of the North Fork, which has its own history of gold mining activity. The towering cliffs of Johannesburg Mountain and Cascade Peak tower above the far side of the valley, rising to neck-stretching heights above the surrounding country. To the northwest is the rocky summit of the Triad, and to the east of it is Eldorado Peak, mantled in glaciers. The path soon ascends into a mature forest of spruce, fir, and hemlock; it zigzags upward at a gradual but ceaseless pace. After climbing high up the wall of the valley, the path swings eastward for the level approach to Cascade Pass. The trees dwindle away here, becoming both smaller in stature and more scattered, allowing fine views of the surrounding peaks. Ahead, Magic Mountain's steep horn is framed by the pass.

Watch for marmots as the trail crosses the final talus slopes and alpine meadows before the pass. Cascade Pass is mantled in verdant meadows punctuated by wind-torn copses of subalpine fir. A viewing bench faces east toward Magic Mountain and Pelton Peak, which flank Yawning Glacier. Farther down the valley is the summit of Glory Mountain. From here, follow the trail back down to the trailhead.

Miles and Directions

0.0 Cascade Pass Trailhead.

2.6 Junction with abandoned Diamond Mine Trail. Bear right.

3.7 Cascade Pass. Turn around.

7.4 Arrive back at Cascade Pass Trailhead.

Ross Lake and the Heart of the North Cascades

Ross Lake National Recreation Area lies at the heart of the North Cascades, splitting the national park into two separate units. The hydroelectric potential of the Skagit River was recognized by early pioneers: A small Pelton-wheel powerhouse was built in 1900 on the current site of Diablo to power a lumber mill. Big corporations soon moved in, and between 1924 and 1961, the Seattle City Light Company impounded the waters of the Skagit River to form Gorge Lake, Diablo Lake, and Ross Lake itself. The company also built a spur railway to aid in the construction of the dams. More than 40 miles of valley was flooded during the creation of these reservoirs, which became the defining features of the landscape.

Although much of the ecologically important bottomland was lost to flooding, the reservoirs have proved to be a boon to recreational visitors. The turquoise waters of Diablo Lake, tinted by the effluvium of melting glaciers, have become a popular spot for power boaters, with campgrounds along the shore for backcountry stays.

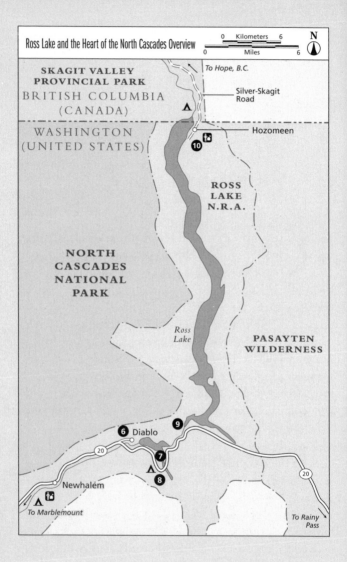

Ross Lake and the Heart of the North Cascades Overview

0   Kilometers   6
0   Miles   6

N

To Hope, B.C.

SKAGIT VALLEY
PROVINCIAL PARK
BRITISH COLUMBIA
(CANADA)

Silver-Skagit
Road

WASHINGTON
(UNITED STATES)

Hozomeen

10

ROSS
LAKE
N.R.A.

NORTH
CASCADES
NATIONAL
PARK

Ross Lake

PASAYTEN
WILDERNESS

Diablo   9

6

20

7

8

Newhalem

20

To Marblemount

To Rainy
Pass

The long and fjord-like finger of Ross Lake projects deep into the heart of the snowcapped peaks, and its lack of an accessible motorboat launch site makes it largely the domain of canoeists and kayakers. Campgrounds with boat landings are scattered at regular intervals along the lake's shores and on its small islands. Plan to paddle during the mornings and evenings; midday winds build up immense swells that make boating both laborious and dangerous.

The easiest access for canoeists is by paddling Diablo Lake from Colonial Campground to its head, then portaging up a 1-mile gravel road to surmount Ross Dam. The Ross Lake Resort will drive your boat up or down this road at prices that reflect their monopoly. The resort also rents canoes by the hour and provides motorboat shuttles to lakeside trailheads. The lakeshore can also be accessed through Hozomeen, after a long drive through Canada that includes 40 miles of gravel forest roads.

Ross Lake National Recreation Area is administered by the National Park Service, and all backcountry and boat-accessed camps require a permit that can be obtained at a permanently staffed ranger station. Beyond the lakeshores, most of the recreation area falls within the Steven Mather Wilderness, and motorized devices and mechanized transportation are prohibited here. In contrast to on the national park lands, pets are allowed throughout the recreation area if they are properly leashed. Please note that mountain bikes are expressly prohibited on all trails within the national park complex, including Ross Lake N.R.A.

Ranger stations at Marblemount and Hozomeen are the primary sources for backcountry information and permits. There is also a Park Service visitor center in Newhalem that offers interpretive displays and multimedia programs. The town of Newhalem is a company town built entirely by Seattle City Light; it has a small general store that is stocked with a few bare essentials. The nearest true grocery and motels are in Marblemount, and for backpacking equipment one must venture even farther down the Skagit Valley to Burlington or Mount Vernon. The Ross Lake Resort offers remote lodgings (but no restaurant) in their complex of floating cabins near Ross Dam.

6 Stetattle Creek

Type of hike: Out-and-back.
Distance: 1.6 miles.
Time required: 45 minutes to 1.5 hours.
Elevation change: Minimal.
Best season: Mid-May to late October.
Maps: USGS Diablo Dam; Green Trails Diablo Lake.
Jurisdiction: Ross Lake National Recreation Area (National Park Service).

Finding the trailhead: From Newhalem, drive east on Washington Highway 20 to mile 126, where a spur road runs into the company town of Diablo. Follow this road and park in the parking lot beside the bridge, just within Diablo. The trail starts on the opposite side of the road.

The Hike

Stetattle Creek marks an ancient tribal boundary. To the Skagit people it was a dangerous hinterland, beyond which was the domain of their enemies the Ntlakyapamuks, or Thompson Indians. Modern visitors can approach the lower reaches of the creek as an easy introduction to the coastal forests of the Cascades; more adventurous souls can penetrate deeper into the hinterlands for a more challenging day trip.

The early reaches of the trail offer an easy stroll along the streambank. As the houses of Diablo fall behind, a riparian woodland closes in around the stream. This diverse forest community includes hemlock, cedar, bigleaf maple, and red alder. The damp climate provides superb growing conditions for epiphytes, plants that grow from aerial perches on the trunks or limbs of trees. Of these, spikemoss is particu-

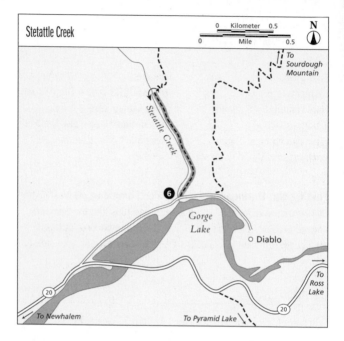

Stetattle Creek

Gorge
Lake

○ Diablo

To
Sourdough
Mountain

To
Ross
Lake

6

20

To Newhalem

To Pyramid Lake

20

larly abundant, and licorice fern can also be found. Watch
the boulders in the stream for the water ouzel, a tiny water-
bird that dives into the current in a quest for aquatic insects.
The bottomland sojourn ends with a series of breath-stealing
switchbacks that carry the trail up the steep slopes to the east
of the creek. This marks the endpoint of the hike. Retrace
the trail back to the trailhead.

7 Thunder Knob

Type of hike: Out-and-back.
Distance: 3.6 miles.
Time required: 2 to 3 hours.
Elevation change: 630-foot gain.
Best season: Mid-April to early November.

Maps: USGS Ross Dam (trail not shown); Green Trails Diablo Lake.
Jurisdiction: Ross Lake National Recreation Area (National Park Service).

Finding the trailhead: Follow Washington Highway 20 to Colonial Campground at mile 130.2, 11 miles east of Newhalem. The trail begins on the north side of the highway, beside the entrance to the north loop of the campground.

The Hike

This wheelchair-accessible trail offers a gentle climb through the trees to reach the top of a wooded promontory above Diablo Lake. The path is rarely far from the highway except near its end, and road noise is a periodic intrusion along most of the route.

The trail begins by passing through the north loop of the Colonial Campground, wandering through a lush forest of Douglas fir and hemlock. It crosses the multiple channels carved out by Colonial Creek during a major flood in 2003. Note the forest floor's lush growth of mosses and ferns. These soon give way to salal and kinnikinnick as the path seeks higher, stony ground where the thin soil offers only enough moisture to sustain lodgepole pine, a fire-dependent tree more typical of the dry side of the Cascades.

The trail zigzags its way upward amid bedrock outcrops, and openings in the trees yield southward views up the

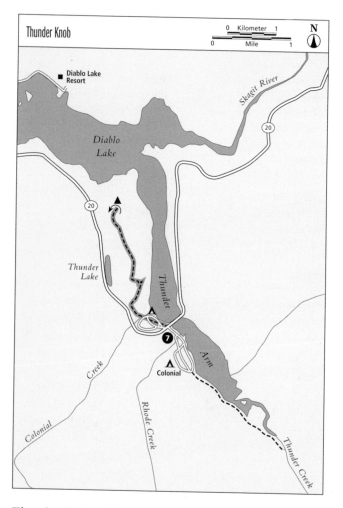

Thunder Creek valley, as well as Colonial Peak to the south-west. The path crests a first high point, then descends to visit some marshy ponds. Note the difference in the forest, which is supported by the moister microclimate found here.

The trail then rises to reach the end of the promontory, where various overlooks yield views of the turquoise waters of Diablo Lake, tinted by the refraction of sunlight through fine suspended sediments known as glacial flour, carried down from glaciers by Thunder Creek. The rounded summit across the reservoir is Huckleberry Mountain, while Jack Mountain is visible to the east and Davis Peak rises prominently above the mouth of Stetattle Creek to the west.

8 Thunder Creek

Type of hike: Out-and-back.
Total distance: 2.9 miles.
Time required: 1.5 to 2.5 hours.
Elevation change: 80-foot gain.
Best season: Mid-April to early November.

Maps: USGS Ross Dam; Green Trails Diablo Lake.
Jurisdiction: Ross Lake National Recreation Area (National Park Service).

Finding the trailhead: Follow Washington Highway 20 to Colonial Campground at mile 130.2, 11 miles east of Newhalem. The trail begins at the south end of the campground, next to the amphitheater.

The Hike

This trail was originally blazed by prospectors bound for the gold-bearing veins along Skagit Queen Creek. A number of hard-rock claims were staked, shafts were blasted into the mountainsides, and by 1905 the first of a series of mining consortiums was incorporated to scratch out fortunes in precious metals from this remote mountain wilderness. Equip-

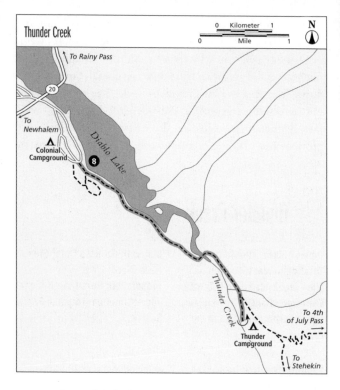

0   Kilometer   1

0   Mile   1

N

To Rainy Pass

20

To
Newhalem

Colonial
Campground

8

Diablo Lake

Thunder Creek

To 4th
of July Pass

Thunder
Campground

To
Stehekin

ment and supplies had to be packed in from Marblemount
by mule train, across the narrow ledges of Devils Elbow,
and through the deep forests that led along the Skagit and
up Thunder Creek itself. But the veins were shallow and
the ore played out quickly, the mining companies went
bankrupt and the prospectors went away penniless, and the
wilderness swallowed up the signs of their vain efforts.

Today, the valley of Thunder Creek offers a long trek
through old-growth conifers. Leave your mountain bike at
the trailhead, and be sure that all pets are properly leashed.

The trek begins by following an arm of Diablo Lake, with periodic views of its turquoise water. This unique coloration is the result of glacial silt, which flows down into the lake from the Boston, Klawatti, and Neve glaciers. Glacial silt is so fine that it floats suspended in the water, refracting light so that only aquamarine colors escape. After 0.9 mile, the trail reaches the mouth of Thunder Creek, where drowned forest dating from the floods of 2003 can be seen. A bridge once sited 3 miles downstream was built in 1913, packed overland piece by piece by mule. Its original site was flooded in 1928 during the construction of Diablo Dam. It is ironic that, in 2003, natural flooding destroyed the footbridge sited here that replaced the historic structure. Now a well-built trail continues up the west bank of the stream, climbing through an old forest where ancient, post–fire Douglas firs are being overtaken by the more shade-tolerant western hemlock. Watch for fern moss on the forest floor. The trail then descends to follow the purling waters of Thunder Creek to the new bridge that leads across the stream to the ancient grove of spruce and hemlock at Thunder Camp.

From Thunder Camp, retrace the trail back to the trail-head at Colonial Campground.

Miles and Directions

0.0 Trailhead in Colonial Campground south unit.

0.6 Junction with Thunder Woods Nature Trail. Stay left for Thunder Creek.

1.4 Bridge leads across Thunder Creek to Thunder Camp. Retrace the trail.

2.9 Arrive back at the trailhead in Colonial Campground.

9 Ross Dam

Type of hike: Out-and-back.
Distance: 2.4 miles.
Time required: 1 to 2 hours.
Elevation change: 530-foot gain.
Best season: Mid-May to early November.

Maps: USGS Ross Dam; Green Trails Ross Lake.
Jurisdiction: Ross Lake National Recreation Area (National Park Service).

Finding the trailhead: The trail begins at the Ross Dam Trailhead at mile 134 on Washington Highway 20, 4 miles east of Colonial Campground.

The Hike

This hike descends to cross Ross Dam and then follows the far shore of the lake to a scenic overlook. The Ross Dam Trailhead sits on a bluff high above the lakeshore, and from its large parking lot, the path wanders downward through storm-wracked Douglas firs. The path passes a small cascade on Happy Creek, then drops across an open and rocky face that yields views of Pyramid Peak to the southwest. The trail bottoms out on a service road; turn left and then right, following signs for Ross Dam. The route then leads across the top of the dam, its curving façade of concrete rising 320 feet above the Skagit River. The dam was constructed in 1937 and flooded the Skagit Valley for 21 miles upstream.

On the far shore, the trail begins a brisk ascent as it turns eastward above the lakeshore. An opening atop this grade yields views of Ruby Mountain to the south as well as a waterfall on the far shore. These falls are not natural but were created when engineers diverted part of Happy Creek

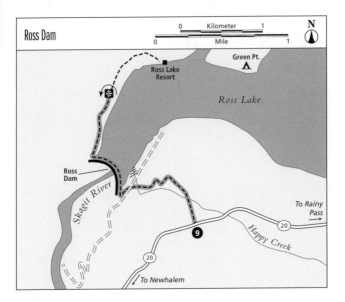

to enter Ross Lake above the dam, thus increasing the water available for hydropower. Turn around here and retrace the trail to complete the hike.

Miles and Directions

0.0 Trailhead above Ross Dam.
0.7 Trail runs out onto dam access road. Turn left.
0.9 Trail crosses Ross Dam and follows the shore of Ross Lake.
1.2 Viewpoint above Ross Lake. Turn around.
2.4 Arrive back at the trailhead.

10 Hozomeen Lake

Type of hike: Out-and-back.
Distance: 7.8 miles.
Time required: 4 to 7 hours.
Elevation change: 1,000-foot gain.
Best season: Early June to mid-August.
Maps: USGS Hozomeen Mountain; Green Trails Ross Lake.
Jurisdiction: Ross Lake National Recreation Area (National Park Service).

Finding the trailhead: Drive north into Canada and follow the Trans-Canada Highway (Route 1) to Hope, British Columbia. From the western edge of town, follow Silver-Skagit Road south for 38 miles to the U.S.–Canada border. This road has a broad, gravel surface that may have numerous potholes and washboards. Once in the United States, drive past the ranger station and take the second left, which accesses a campground loop. The trailhead is at the end of this road, beside a historic customs cabin.

The Hike

This hike offers a long day trip to a lowland lake below the striking crags of Hozomeen Mountain. It is a popular day hike for visitors who find themselves in the Hozomeen area. Heavy concentrations of mosquitoes plague the area between mid–August and mid–October.

The trail begins beside a historic customs cabin and ascends briskly through the timber above the Hozomeen Campground. The forest soon thins to become a sparse growth of spindly Douglas firs and lodgepole pines, the sure sign of an old burn. The thin and stony soil is covered with mosses and foliose lichens, which are related to the caribou moss of the Arctic tundra.

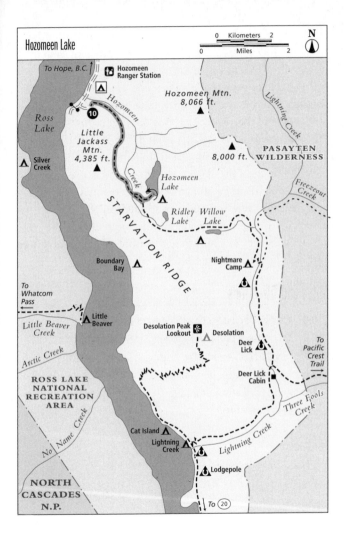

At the top of the initial grade, the trail reaches a level upland where stately cedars grow. The gradient is gentler now, and it remains so as far as the junction with the spur path to Hozomeen Lake. This side trail leads 0.6 miles through a broad watershed divide to reach the lake, a vast lowland pool that lies at the foot of Hozomeen Mountain. *Hozomeen* means "sharp like a knife" in the dialect of the Ntlakyapamuks, or Thompson Indians. This description is well-suited to the several sheer crags that rise from the massif. Mule deer are abundant (and sometimes pestiferous) here, and loons are commonly spotted on the still waters. There is a pretty campground at the south end of the lake, and visitors will find fair fishing for trout. Turn around here and retrace the trail to complete the hike.

Miles and Directions

- **0.0** Trailhead at old Hozomeen customs cabin.
- **3.0** Trail crosses Hozomeen Creek.
- **3.1** Junction with spur trail to Hozomeen Lake. Turn left.
- **3.9** Hozomeen Lake. Turn around.
- **7.8** Arrive back at the trailhead.

Rainy Pass and the Cascades Divide

As Washington Highway 20 nears the crest of the Cascades, it enters a region of stark granite pinnacles and dense forests that thrive on frequent rains and fogs. The highway crosses two divides here. As you approach from the west, Rainy Pass leads into the valley of Bridge Creek, a tributary of the Stehekin River that ultimately pours its waters into Lake Chelan. Farther east is the even higher divide of Washington Pass, where the Early Winters Spires guard the rim of the Methow River watershed, which drains eastward into the Columbia River. The ranges surrounding the road offer some of the most awe-inspiring scenery in the North Cascades. These are prime recreation lands; the timber is so spindly here that loggers have never bothered with it, and the rather marginal lodes of precious metals played out years ago. Nonetheless, the lands surrounding Rainy Pass were inexplicably declared to be unfit for national park status. Today, the area falls within an unprotected portion of the Okanogan National Forest, and the Forest Service has thus far done a fine job of protecting the wild character of the landscape.

The landscape here is defined by a geologic feature known as the Golden Horn Batholith. *Batholith* is Latin for "sea of stone"; the formation originated millions of years

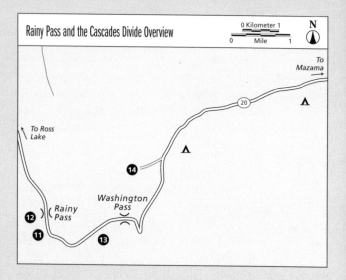

Rainy Pass and the Cascades Divide Overview

0 Kilometer 1

0 Mile 1

N

To Mazama →

20

To Ross Lake

14

Washington Pass

12) Rainy Pass

11

13

ago as a huge upwelling of molten rock that rose through faults in the Earth's crust as it cooled below the surface. As the magma cooled and hardened into granitic rock, it contracted, and vertical cracks or joints developed. These joints weakened the stone, and over the course of eons, frost shattering has exploited the vertical weaknesses in the rock. Thus, erosion has chiseled away at the great batholith to create towering walls and sharp needles of stone. As the Golden Horn granite cooled, some of the cracks in the newly forged bedrock were infused with mineral-rich, superheated water. This process resulted in the formation of veins of quartz in the bedrock, and some of these veins contained substantial quantities of gold and silver. These mother lodes became the basis of a small gold rush that occurred here in the late 1880s.

To the north of Rainy Pass is the Pasayten Wilderness,

a vast sea of sedimentary peaks. It has a more continental climate than is found to the west of the divide, with hotter summers and colder, drier winters. Lowland forests are typically dominated by Douglas fir, with dense stands of lodgepole pine or open savannas of ponderosa pine in drier areas where wildfires are a dominant force in shaping the landscape. Near the timberline, Engelmann spruce and subalpine fir are the dominant trees, while whitebark pine is prevalent in arid areas. Stands of subalpine larch can be found in some of the highest and most windswept locales. The alpine meadows above the treeline are typified by a greater number of grasses and fewer flowering plants than are found farther west, although there can be stunning displays of wildflowers in locales that receive plenty of moisture.

Rainy Pass can be reached easily via the North Cascades Highway (WA 20). Services near Rainy Pass are nonexistent: the nearest place to get gas and supplies is Mazama, down on the Methow River. It is 11 miles farther east to Winthrop, the first real town. Traveling west from Rainy Pass, it is 38 miles to the company store at Newhalem and an additional 13 miles to Marblemount for gas and groceries. Forest Service campgrounds on WA 20 can be found 6 miles east of Washington Pass, and westbound travelers will have to drive 27 miles from Rainy Pass to reach Colonial Campground, which is run by the Park Service. For more information, stop in at the Forest Service visitor center in Winthrop.

11 Rainy Lake

Type of hike: Out-and-back.
Distance: 1.8 miles.
Time required: 45 minutes to 1.5 hours.
Elevation change: Minimal.

Best season: Late June to mid-October.
Topo Maps: Green Trails Washington Pass.
Jurisdiction: Okanogan National Forest.

Finding the trailhead: The trail departs from the Rainy Pass picnic area at mile 157 on Washington Highway 20.

The Hike

This short, paved trail starts at Rainy Pass and contours along the mountainsides to enter the glacier-carved cirque that bears Rainy Lake and the impressive waterfall that feeds it. This is a short, level trek that is well-suited to wheelchairs. There are a few interpretive signs scattered in the forest along the trail.

The trail begins in a series of subalpine bogs and meadows, where Engelmann spruce have taken root in the cool, damp soil. As the trail nears the halfway point, a pleasant series of waterfalls tumbles down through the forest, draining the waters of Lake Ann in a hanging valley high above. The forest is now dominated by silver fir and mountain hemlock; watch for the blossoms of fairy bells, violets, and queen's cup lilies in the understory, as well as the delicate fronds of ferns.

At the end of the trail is a viewpoint at the foot of Rainy Lake. Its brilliant turquoise waters are fed by an impressive waterfall that descends from the Lyall Glacier. The towering

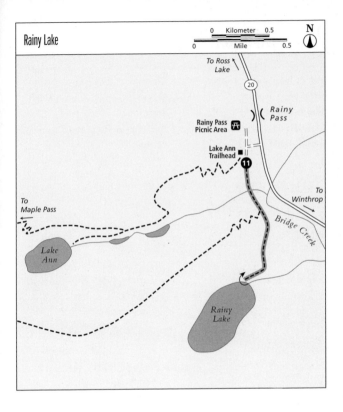

crags of Frisco Mountain rise above the head of the basin. There is a fine population of husky cutthroats in the lake, but the brushy lakeshores make fishing difficult without a boat. Turn around here to complete the hike.

12 Lake Ann

Type of hike: Out-and-back.
Distance: 3.8 miles.
Time required: 2 to 3.5 hours.
Elevation change: 720-foot gain.
Best season: Late July to early October.

Maps: Green Trails Washington Pass.
Jurisdiction: Okanogan National Forest.

Finding the trailhead: The trail departs from the Rainy Pass picnic area at mile 157 on Washington Highway 20.

The Hike

This trail climbs from Rainy Pass to Lake Ann, a pleasant cirque lake surrounded by steep cliffs and slender waterfalls. It offers a wilder and slightly more challenging alternative to the Rainy Lake Trail.

From the parking lot at Rainy Pass, the trail zigzags upward through a mature subalpine forest. The path soon turns south, traversing around the edge of a small bowl. Several avalanche paths face eastward toward the sharp spires of Stiletto Peak. Talus slopes soon drop away into the grassy floor of the basin, where marmots are often spotted among the boulders. As the path traverses onto the south wall of the basin, sparsely timbered slopes offer excellent northward views. From right to left, the prominent summits are Whistler Mountain, Cutthroat Peak, and Tower Mountain.

The trail then strikes Lake Ann's outlet stream at a fine waterfall and follows it into a hanging valley carved by glaciers. The spur path to Lake Ann soon descends to the left. It runs through the timbered lower reaches of the basin, then breaks out into open country dotted with snowmelt

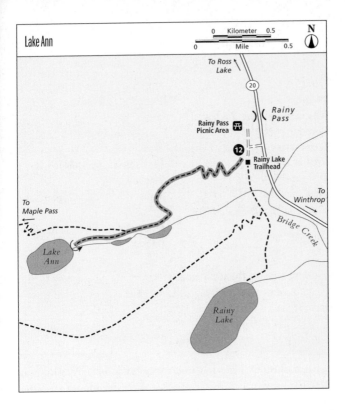

Lake Ann

0   Kilometer   0.5

0   Mile   0.5

N

To Ross Lake

20

Rainy Pass

Rainy Pass Picnic Area

12

Rainy Lake Trailhead

To Winthrop

To Maple Pass

Bridge Creek

Lake Ann

Rainy Lake

ponds and wet meadows. Look backward as you approach the lake for views of the Early Winters Spires. The lake itself is bordered by low but rocky peaks that bear several small waterfalls down into the basin. Anglers will find fair fishing for undersize cutthroat trout. Turn around here and retrace the trail to complete the hike.

Miles and Directions

0.0 Rainy Pass Day Use Area. Follow Maple Pass Trail.

1.4 Junction with trail to Lake Ann. Turn left.

1.9 Lake Ann. Turn around.

3.8 Arrive back at the trailhead.

13   Blue Lake

Type of hike: Out-and-back.
Distance: 4.4 miles.
Time required: 2 to 4 hours.
Elevation change: 1,050-foot gain.

Best season: Mid-July to mid-October.
Maps: Green Trails Washington Pass.
Jurisdiction: Okanogan National Forest.

Finding the trailhead: The trail leaves from a parking area to the south of Washington Highway 20 at mile 161, 1 mile west of Washington Pass.

The Hike

This trail offers a modest trek in the vicinity of Washington Pass, climbing into the larches of the timberline to reach a deep lake surrounded by impressive walls and pinnacles of granite. The trail begins by running eastward through the subalpine forest beside the highway. It soon turns south, climbing moderately through a sparse growth of large mountain hemlocks. Gaps in the trees offer early views across Washington Pass; the tawny summit is Cutthroat Peak. About halfway to the lake, the trail breaks out of the trees onto old rockslides that are now mantled in meadows and fringed by subalpine larches. These unique conifers their turn brilliant gold before shedding needles in late October.

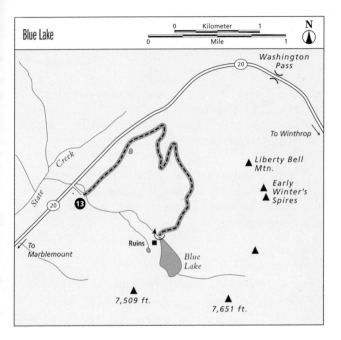

The surrounding peaks are now unveiled, stretching westward to include Mount Hardy and Black Peak.

The trail now ascends gradually on a westward course,
and the summit of Liberty Bell Mountain uncloaks itself to
the east, flanked by the Early Winters Spires. Near the trail's
end, a rushing stream leads upward to the rocky shores of
Blue Lake. This deep alpine tarn is guarded by imposing
rock walls, and its translucent waters are home to an abundance of cutthroat trout. Camping is no longer allowed here
due to the heavy impacts of past visitors on the fragile larch-
heather community of the lakeshore. Turn around here and
retrace the trail to complete the hike.

14 Cutthroat Lake

Type of hike: Out-and-back.
Distance: 2.8 miles.
Time required: 1.5 to 2.5 hours.
Elevation change: 410-foot gain.
Best season: Late June to mid-October.

Maps: Green Trails Washington Pass.
Jurisdiction: Okanogan National Forest.

Finding the trailhead: From Washington Pass, drive east on Washington Highway 20 for 4.5 miles to Cutthroat Creek Road. Follow this paved road west for 1.5 miles to reach the trailhead and the camping area at its end.

The Hike

This wide and well-engineered trail makes an easy day hike to Cutthroat Lake. Because the sensitive heather parks that line the lakeshores are extremely susceptible to damage, camping is forbidden within a quarter mile of the shoreline. Hikers who seek a more challenging trek can follow the steady but moderate grade that climbs to reach the crest of the divide at Cutthroat Pass.

The trek begins by crossing a bridge over Cutthroat Creek and climbing gently through an open woodland of Douglas fir and lodgepole pine. This entire valley burned around the turn of the twentieth century, and the resulting forest is composed of fire-resistant and fire-dependent plant species. All along the way there are fine views of the tawny crags of sedimentary rock that line the valley. As the trail continues upward, it passes through several isolated groves of spruce that were spared by the blaze. These groves rep-

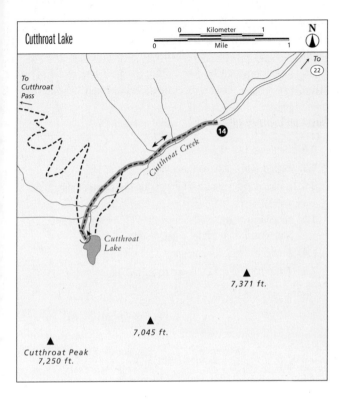

Cutthroat Lake

Cutthroat Creek

14

To
Cutthroat
Pass

To
22

Cutthroat
Lake

▲
7,371 ft.

▲
7,045 ft.

▲
Cutthroat Peak
7,250 ft.

resent the pre-fire forest community that once covered the valley floor.

After 0.9 mile of traveling, the first spur path to Cutthroat Lake leads westward across hummocky parks to reach the eastern shore. A short distance farther on, the main trail splits, and the left fork leads to the north shore of the lake. Ringed by an open woodland of mountain hemlock and subalpine larch, the green waters of Cutthroat Lake are guarded on two sides by rugged mountains, the tallest of which is Cutthroat Peak. The lake is quite shallow, and as it fills in with silt, meadows take over where the fish once swam. Anglers will find fair fishing for pan-size trout. Turn around here and retrace the trail to complete the hike.

Miles and Directions

0.0 Cutthroat Lake Trailhead.

0.1 Bridge over Cutthroat Creek.

0.9 Junction with spur trail. Turn left for east shore of lake (0.5 mile).

1.3 Junction with trail to Cutthroat Pass (3.2 miles, moderately strenuous). Turn left for outlet of lake.

1.4 Cutthroat Lake. Turn around.

2.8 Arrive back at the Cutthroat Lake Trailhead.

Harts Pass and the Pasayten Wilderness

The vast and remote Pasayten Wilderness stretches eastward from the crest of the Cascades to encompass arid ranges and wooded basins, untamed rivers and peaceful alpine lakes. Overshadowed by the national park lands to the west, the Pasayten receives relatively few visitors. It is vast in extent, more than half a million acres in all. One can literally hike for weeks here without crossing a road or one's own tracks. There are also a number of fine day hikes along the southern edge of the wilderness for visitors who lack the time or inclination for a prolonged journey.

The mountains to the east of the Cascade crest have a more continental climate than is found to the west of the divide, with hotter summers and colder, drier winters. Lowland forests are typically populated by Douglas fir, with dense stands of lodgepole pine or open savannas of ponderosa pine in drier areas where wildfires are a significant force in shaping the landscape. Near the timberline, Engelmann spruce and subalpine fir are the dominant trees, while whitebark pine is prevalent in arid areas. Stands of subalpine larch can be found in some of the highest and most wind-swept locales. The alpine meadows above the treeline are typified by a greater number of grasses and fewer flowering plants than are found farther west, although there can be

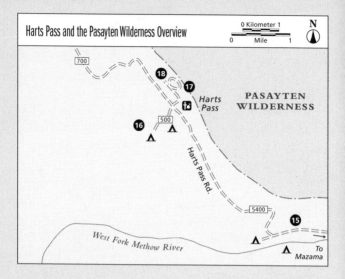

0 Kilometer 1

0 Mile 1

N

700

18

17

Harts Pass

PASAYTEN
WILDERNESS

500

16

Harts Pass Rd.

5400

15

West Fork Methow River

To
Mazama

stunning displays of wildflowers in areas that receive plenty of moisture.

The Pasayten is truly a multiple-use wilderness. It is popular with horse parties, and a few trunk trails receive heavy use by horse traffic. The area has been used as a summer range for domestic sheep since the early 1900s, and grazing is still permitted in some parts of the wilderness. Some of the alpine lakes provide outstanding fishing for trout, and the neighboring Methow River is also well-known for its fly fishing. In late September, hunters stalk the ridges and streams of the Pasayten in pursuit of deer. Travelers who enter the Pasayten country at this time should wear blaze orange clothing. During the winter months, the Methow Valley is a mecca for cross-country skiing, but the steep country of the Pasayten itself is too avalanche-prone for backcountry ski trips.

Backcountry permits are not required, although there is a new fee for each night of parking on the national forest lands that surround the wilderness. The fees are part of an experimental pilot program; be sure to voice your opinions about the fees to your congressional representatives.

The main access route to the Pasayten is Harts Pass Road (Forest Road 5400), which runs 18.5 miles from Mazama to Harts Pass, near the timberline. The road is wide and well maintained through the Methow River valley, but it becomes narrow and steep as it climbs the valley walls and winds up past Deadhorse Point to reach the high country to the west. Potholes and fallen rocks can make for challenging driving, particularly for vehicles with low clearance. From Harts Pass, a good road winds up toward Slate Peak, and a narrow and rutted track descends along Slate Creek to end at the Cady Pass Trailhead, where the road has been washed out and abandoned (Chancellor Campground can no longer be reached by car).

There is little in the way of services near the Pasayten Wilderness. Gas and limited supplies can be obtained at the small mercantile store in Mazama. Eleven miles east of Mazama is the resort town of Winthrop, where visitors will find backpacking supplies, excellent restaurants, bed-and-breakfast lodgings, and a laid-back atmosphere that harkens back to the days of the Old West. Travelers who seek a more rustic experience will find several Forest Service campgrounds along the West Fork of the Methow as well as two pretty campgrounds in the vicinity of Harts Pass. There is a Forest Service visitor center in Winthrop, and a ranger cabin at Harts Pass is staffed sporadically during the summer months.

15 Beauty Creek Falls

Type of hike: Out-and-back.
Distance: 5.9 miles.
Time required: 3 to 5 hours.
Elevation change: 940-foot gain.
Best season: Mid-May to mid-October.

Maps: USFS Pasayten Wilderness; USGS Robinson Mountain; Green Trails Washington Pass.
Jurisdiction: Pasayten Wilderness (Okanogan National Forest).

Finding the trailhead: Take Washington Highway 20 to the Mazama cutoff road, 11 miles west of Winthrop. After a mile, there is a T intersection. Turn left, passing the Mazama general store. This is Harts Pass Road (Forest Road 5400), which is paved as far as the Lost River, about 5 miles. Turn right onto a spur road at mile 7 to reach the trek's beginning at the Robinson Creek Trailhead.

The Hike

This valley-bottom trail follows Robinson Creek into the Pasayten Wilderness. The roaring waterfall on Beauty Creek makes an excellent day-hike destination and is open in early summer when the high country is still locked in snow.

The trek begins at the mouth of Robinson Creek as the trail runs north through a bottomland forest of Douglas fir and ponderosa pine typical of the dry side of the Cascades. After a short distance, the path climbs heartily up the mountainside to attain an altitude that is several hundred feet above the valley floor. A split waterfall is visible from the brushy slopes, and across the valley are the cliff bands of Scramble Point. The trail ultimately levels off, and the valley floor rises to meet it. The path crosses the Pasayten Wilderness boundary in a floodplain stand of cottonwood, Douglas fir, and western red cedar.

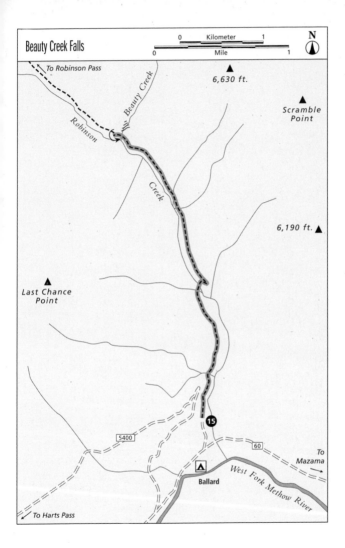

Beauty Creek Falls

N

0   Kilometer   1
0   Mile   1

To Robinson Pass

Beauty Creek

▲ 6,630 ft.

▲ Scramble Point

Robinson

Creek

6,190 ft. ▲

▲ Last Chance Point

15

5400

60

To Mazama →

Ballard

West Fork Methow River

← To Harts Pass

A bridge soon spans the rushing waters of Robinson Creek, offering the first views of Last Chance Point with its broad apron of talus and castellated crown of surreal spires and cockscombs. The trail crosses brushfields dominated by an aromatic shrub known as ceanothus, then reaches a stout bridge over Beauty Creek. A spectacular waterfall tumbles down the cliffs here, and a short distance beyond it, an unmarked spur runs to the edge of a picturesque gorge chiseled into the bedrock by Robinson Creek. Turn around here and retrace the trail to complete the hike.

Miles and Directions

- **0.0** Robinson Creek Trailhead.
- **1.0** Trail enters the Pasayten Wilderness.
- **1.2** Trail crosses Robinson Creek and follows north bank.
- **2.9** Trail crosses Beauty Creek below a large waterfall. Turn around.
- **5.9** Arrive back at the trailhead.

16 Trout Creek Divide

Type of hike: Out-and-back.
Distance: 8.8 miles.
Time required: 4 to 7 hours.
Elevation change: 905-foot gain.
Best season: Late July to early
October.

Maps: USFS Pasayten Wilderness; USGS Slate Peak; Green Trails Washington Pass.
Jurisdiction: Okanogan National Forest.

Finding the trailhead: Take Washington Highway 20 to the Mazama cutoff road, 11 miles west of Winthrop. After a mile, there is a T intersection. Turn left, passing the Mazama general store. This is Harts Pass Road (Forest Road 5400), which is paved as far as the Lost River, about 5 miles. It then becomes gravel, and is narrow and winding with many potholes as it makes the steep climb past Deadhorse Point toward Harts Pass. Just before reaching the pass, turn left onto Forest Road 5400-500, following signs for the Meadows Campground. Follow this improved gravel road for 2 miles to its end to reach the trailhead.

The Hike

This segment of the Pacific Crest Trail follows the high ridgetops southward from Harts Pass, yielding excellent views before it drops toward Glacier Pass. It then follows Brush Creek to the West Fork of the Methow River. The low divide known informally as "Grasshopper Pass" lies just across the valley from Azurite Peak, and its larch-studded meadows make an ideal destination for day hikers.

The trail begins above the old Brown Bear Mine, ascending moderately across a steep and rocky bowl. Marmots, pikas, and golden-mantled ground squirrels are abundant here, and a few subalpine larches rise from rocky

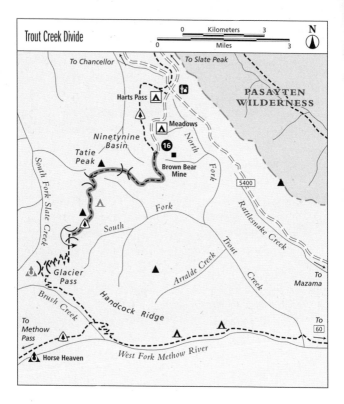

Kilometers

Miles

PASAYTEN WILDERNESS

To Chancellor

To Slate Peak

Harts Pass

Meadows

Ninetynine Basin

Tatie Peak

16

Brown Bear Mine

North Fork

5400

South Fork Slate Creek

South Fork

Trout Creek

Rattlesnake Creek

Arralde Creek

To Mazama

Glacier Pass

Handcock Ridge

Brush Creek

To Methow Pass

To 60

Horse Heaven

West Fork Methow River

moorings at the edge of the talus. The prominent massif to the east is Robinson Mountain. The upthrust strata of a rocky peak rise ahead, and the trail rises to surmount the ridgetop to the east of its summit.

Emerging high above the South Fork of Trout Creek, the trail offers a spectacular vista of the granite peaks of the Golden Horn Batholith. Gardiner and Silver Star Mountains rise along the eastern edge of the Cascades, with the Needles to the right of them. The craggy spires of Tower Mountain and the Golden Horn are next in line, followed by the distant and snowy summits of Ragged Ridge. A low gap at the head of the South Fork basin reveals the stark summit of Azurite Peak, with its permanent collar of snow.

The trail now embarks upon a high circuit of the basin, crossing flower-studded meadows and arid slopes of shattered stone. A nameless summit guards the head of the basin, and an anticline, or downwarping of the rock strata, can be seen clearly in its east face. A shallow grade leads up to a saddle above the Ninetynine Basin, with its rainbow-banded peaks guarding a collection of shallow ponds in the meadows far below. Views from this point encompass the barren summits of the Pasayten Wilderness stretching northward to the horizon. A gentle descent leads to a pass above the Slate Creek watershed, and a short side trip to the top of the divide yields a stunning perspective of Mount Ballard as well as a distant view of Jack Mountain.

The path now skirts the base of the next summit, passing through sparse stands of larch and crossing broad talus slopes. There are several camps in sheltered spots along the way, with lingering snowfields nearby to supply drinking water. On the far side of the peak, the trail rises onto the long ridgetop known as "Grasshopper Pass," with its larch meadows and face-to-face views of Azurite Peak and Mount Ballard. The rusty tint on the ridge that links the two peaks is derived from the oxidation of iron-rich ores in the bedrock. Turn around here and retrace the trail to complete the hike.

Miles and Directions

0.0   Trailhead. Connecting trail leads upward.

0.1   Junction with Pacific Crest Trail. Turn left to begin hike.

0.7   Trail crosses divide to enter Trout Creek watershed.

4.4   Trail reaches divide opposite Azurite Peak. Turn around.

8.8   Arrive back at the trailhead.

17   Robinson Pass

Type of hike: Out-and-back.
Distance: 10.2 miles.
Time required: 5 to 8.5 hours.
Elevation change: 1,290-foot gain.
Best season: Mid-July to mid-October.

Maps: USFS Pasayten Wilderness; Green Trails Washington Pass.
Jurisdiction: Pasayten Wilderness (Okanogan National Forest).

Finding the trailhead: Take Washington Highway 20 to the Mazama cutoff road, 11 miles west of Winthrop. After a mile, there is a T intersection. Turn left, passing the Mazama general store. This is Harts Pass Road (Forest Road 5400), which is paved as far as the Lost River, about 5 miles. It then becomes gravel, and is narrow and winding with many potholes as it makes the steep climb past Deadhorse Point to reach Harts Pass, 18.5 miles beyond Mazama. Turn right onto Forest Road 5400-600 and follow it 1.8 miles to the trailhead at the second switchback, which is the Slate Pass Trailhead.

The Hike

This trek follows a little-used connecting trail that links Slate Pass with Robinson Creek via a gem-like but nameless saddle. There are several unmarked intersections along the

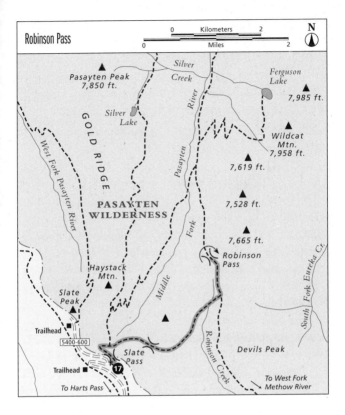

Kilometers 0 2
Miles 0 2

N

Silver Creek

Pasayten Peak
7,850 ft.

Ferguson
Lake

7,985 ft.

Silver
Lake

GOLD RIDGE

West Fork Pasayten River

Pasayten River

Wildcat
Mtn.
7,958 ft.

7,619 ft.

PASAYTEN
WILDERNESS

7,528 ft.

Middle Fork

7,665 ft.

Robinson
Pass

Haystack
Mtn.

South Fork Eureka Cr.

Slate
Peak

Trailhead

5400-600

Robinson Creek

Devils Peak

Trailhead

17

Slate
Pass

To Harts Pass

To West Fork
Methow River

way, and the trail may be somewhat challenging for novices to follow beyond the nameless pass. Nonetheless, the alpine meadows are beautiful, with impressive wildflower displays and fine views of the barren peaks that rise within the Pasayten Wilderness.

From the Slate Pass Trailhead, follow the Buckskin Ridge Trail for the brief climb over the ridgetop. The trail then descends into a meadowy bowl lined with talus slopes. Marmots are abundant here, and there are eastward views of Devils Peak and Robinson Mountain. At the bottom of the bowl, the trail skirts a copse of larches and a faint track runs eastward toward a nameless saddle. Turn right onto this trail, angling downhill across boulderfields, meadows, and timbered slopes to reach the broad, waterlogged lawns of the pass. Follow the cairns across the verdant swards of wildflowers to reach the far end of the gap, where the path angles northeast onto stony slopes.

The trail now descends across the sparsely timbered slopes of a nameless summit; some route-finding skill is helpful here as the trail is a bit faint in places. The loose woodland is interrupted frequently by shelves of bedrock, and there are fine views down the valley of Robinson Creek, with Devils Peak presiding above its north side. After a rather gentle descent, there is a shallow ford of Robinson Creek, after which the trail climbs to join the Robinson Pass Trail.

Turn left as this well-beaten track climbs out of the old-growth subalpine firs and into a broad series of rolling alpine meadows guarded by Devils Peak. The path climbs moderately to reach the boggy flats of Robinson Pass. The summit faces westward, and one can look out across the valley of the Middle Fork of the Pasayten River. Gold Ridge rises beyond it, with Slate Peak, Haystack Mountain, and Pasayten Peak rising from its meadowy shoulders. Turn around here and retrace the trail to complete the hike.

Miles and Directions

0.0 Slate Pass Trailhead. Follow the Buckskin Ridge Trail upward.

0.1 Slate Pass.

0.6	Unmarked junction with faint trail to Robinson Creek. Turn right.
1.4	Trail crosses through nameless pass to enter Robinson Creek drainage.
3.0	Trail crosses Robinson Creek.
3.2	Junction with Robinson Creek Trail. Turn left.
5.1	Robinson Pass. Turn around.
10.2	Arrive back at trailhead.

18 Tamarack Peak

Type of hike: Out-and-back.
Distance: 8.2 miles.
Time required: 4 to 7 hours.
Elevation change: 640-foot gain.
Best season: Mid-July to mid-October.

Maps: USFS Pasayten Wilderness; USGS Slate Peak, USGS Pasayten Peak; Green Trails Washington Pass, Green Trails Pasayten Peak.
Jurisdiction: Pasayten Wilderness (Okanogan National Forest).

Finding the trailhead: Take Washington Highway 20 to the Mazama cutoff road, 11 miles west of Winthrop. After a mile, there is a T intersection. Turn left, passing the Mazama general store. This is Harts Pass Road (Forest Road 5400), which is paved as far as the Lost River, about 5 miles. It then becomes gravel, and is narrow and winding with many potholes as it makes the steep climb past Deadhorse Point to reach Harts Pass, 18.5 miles beyond Mazama. Turn right onto Forest Road 5400-600 and follow it 1.5 miles to the Slate Peak Pacific Crest Trail Trailhead.

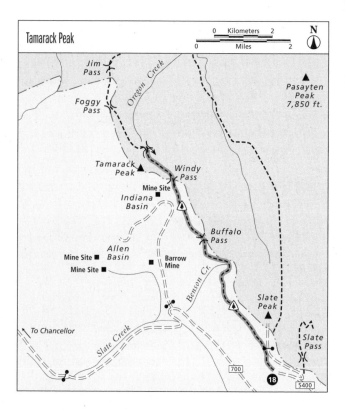

The Hike

This hike follows a section of the Pacific Crest Trail across ridgetop meadows. A sea of barren peaks stretches to the far horizons, and brilliant constellations of mountain wildflowers border the trail. Along the way, the trail visits the Indiana Basin, a historic gold-mining district that dates from the 1890s.

The trek begins with a moderate climb through the alpine meadows on the shoulder of Slate Peak. The summit of the peak is visible ahead, crowned with a fire lookout tower. During the Cold War, the top of the peak was razed and flattened to make space for a radar installation; when the new fire lookout was built on the site, it was built so that the floor of the cabin was at the altitude of the original summit.

The trail levels off as it traverses northward across the steep and open slopes of the peak. Lupine and paintbrush bloom in the moist meadows, while the drier slopes are home to phlox and cinquefoil. Panoramic westward views encompass the heart of the North Cascades. The dominant summit amid a crowd of peaks to the southwest is Mount Ballard. Due west, the two snowy peaks are Crater and Jack Mountains. As the trail continues northward, the distant volcanic cone of Mount Baker, clad eternally in ice and snow, appears between Crater and Jack Mountains.

The path soon crosses the shallow, grassy basin that bears the headwaters of Benson Creek. It then makes its way over a meadowy shoulder of the mountain, unveiling views of the extensive mine workings of the Indiana Basin. During the late 1800s, miners worked their way upstream from the placer gold deposits of Canyon Creek, seeking the mother lode. Alec Barron found the lode in this basin in 1891, igniting a boom of hard-rock mining in the area. Shafts were blasted into the heart of the mountain as miners followed the veins of quartz and gold that made up the mother lode. Enormous heaps of waste rock, called tailings, were piled beneath the portals of the shafts, and they can still be seen today.

The path descends to cross through Windy Pass to enter the Pasayten Wilderness, then traverses the east-facing slopes beyond. There are now views of the barren ridge of crags that rise beyond the West Fork of the Pasayten. The tallest of the crags is Pasayten Peak. The rocky summit that rises above the trail is Tamarack Peak, named for the abundance of "tamarack," or subalpine larch, on its northern slopes. The path soon zigzags up to a high saddle behind a rocky spur of the peak for a final, glorious view of the peaks to the west. Turn around here and retrace the trail to complete the hike.

Miles and Directions

0.0   Slate Peak Pacific Crest Trail Trailhead.

3.5   Trail crosses through Windy Pass and enters Pasayten Wilderness.

4.1   Trail reaches high col behind Tamarack Peak. Turn around.

8.2   Arrive back at Slate Peak Pacific Crest Trail Trailhead.

Lake Chelan and the Stehekin Valley

The deep, blue waters of Lake Chelan extend for more than 50 miles from the semi-arid grasslands of the Columbia Basin into the heart of the North Cascades. About 17,000 years ago, the valley that now holds the lake was occupied by a river of glacial ice, which gouged the deep and narrow basin here today. At the deepest point, the waters of Lake Chelan go down more than 1,500 feet.

Long before the North Cascades Highway was completed in 1972, centuries before miners flooded the valley of Ruby Creek and forged a path over Harts Pass to the north, the native peoples who lived along the shores of Lake Chelan were traveling well-worn trails along a rushing river that poured down from the high peaks and dumped its water at the head of the lake. To the native peoples, the river was *Stehekin,* "the way through." In 1814 Alexander Ross, accompanied by native guides, followed the Stehekin River to Cascades Pass and crossed the mountains in order to assess the region's fur potential for the Hudson Bay Company.

The fur trade never became very profitable here, and the North Cascades remained a backwater. The next big boom came in the late 1880s, when gold was discovered in the region, bringing an influx of rough-cut prospectors who blasted mine shafts into the mountains that guarded

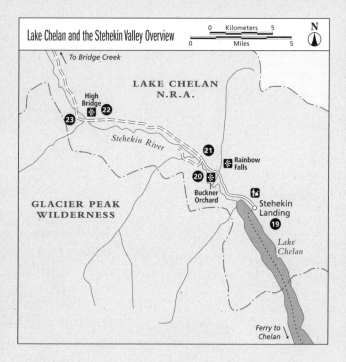

the Stehekin. This boom also faded quickly, giving way to a trickle of hardy settlers who carved homesteads out of the forested bottomlands of the Stehekin Valley. Human settlement has always been sparse, but the valley has been inhabited steadily over the last century by a self-reliant breed of subsistence farmers. Their current year-round population numbers about seventy.

In 1968 the Stehekin Valley was incorporated into the national park complex as the Lake Chelan National Recreation Area. Under the auspices of the National Park Service, this area has become a world-class destination for hikers and refugees from urban turmoil. Hikers will find weather that is typically warmer and drier than that found to the west of the North Cascades; summer temperatures around 90 degrees Fahrenheit are a common occurrence. Mountain weather is still unpredictable, though, and travelers should be prepared for chilly or wet weather, which may strike without warning. Ticks are a rather troublesome pest in the Stehekin Valley and are particularly abundant in spring and early summer. Rattlesnakes also live here, but they are shy and reclusive and rarely present a real danger. Watch where you walk, and if you encounter a rattlesnake, remain still so it can retreat safely.

Stehekin's quaint charm depends upon its remoteness: The only cars in the area were brought in by barge over Lake Chelan. A passenger ferry known as the *Lady of the Lake* plies the water, linking the town of Chelan with the isolated outposts and Forest Service trailheads along the lakeshore. The express boat takes two hours one-way to Stehekin and makes no stops along the way. The regular ferry, which takes four hours one-way, stops at Lucerne and also will make flag stops upon request. Driving 17 miles up the west shore of Lake Chelan to get on the boat at Fields Landing shaves an hour off the transit time. Long-term parking goes for exorbitant rates at either loading location. A note to campers: Stove fuel is officially prohibited on the ferry—don't try to walk onto the boat with a jerry can of white gas. The store in Stehekin does sell white gas by the bottle.

The ferry landing in Stehekin offers a lodge with a restaurant, a camp store, and a small sporting goods concern. A visit to the Golden West Visitor Center, run by the National Park Service, is a must for travelers arriving in Stehekin and trying to get oriented. Camping along the Stehekin Valley

Road requires a free backcountry permit, which can be obtained at the visitor center. There is a bakery up the road a few miles that is not to be missed, and even farther north is the Courtney Guest Ranch, where lodging and meals can be had (reservations required). The Courtney family also runs short horse trips into the park. The Buckner Orchard, across from Rainbow Falls, is a historic fruit orchard established in 1912 and now maintained by the Park Service as a historical attraction for all. The apples ripen in late September and are free to anyone who can coexist with the black bears that also feed there.

From the boat landing, a tour bus runs up-valley for a brief stop at Rainbow Falls. A longer hiker shuttle once ran the 22-mile length of Stehekin Valley Road for a small fee, providing access to trailheads. Floods washed out part of this road in the winter of 1995-96 and again a decade later; as of this writing the shuttle buses were turning around at High Bridge.

19 Chelan Lakeshore

Type of hike: Out-and-back.
Distance: 10.0 miles.
Time required: 2 to 8 hours, depending on destination.
Elevation change: 500-foot gain.
Best season: Mid-April to early November.

Maps: USGS Stehekin, USGS Sun Mountain; Green Trails Stehekin.
Jurisdiction: Lake Chelan National Recreation Area (National Park Service); Lake Chelan–Sawtooth Wilderness (Wenatchee National Forest).

Finding the trailhead: From the Stehekin boat landing, follow unmarked roads south past the Golden West Visitor Center and the fire cache to reach the marked beginning of the trail (about 70 yards).

The Hike

This trail follows the eastern shore of Lake Chelan from the Stehekin visitor center all the way to the mouth of Prince Creek. The lakeshore along this trail was heavily damaged in 2007 during the Flick Creek Fire, which burned 8,000 acres of timber after being ignited by an illegal campfire. This description covers only the first 5 miles of the trail, which offer the best scenery and are visited most often. The first 3.7 miles of the trail fall within Park Service jurisdiction and are quite level. For the easiest option, use Flick Creek camp as a turnaround point. The Flick Creek camping area requires a permit for overnight stays. Beyond the Park Service boundary the path travels through the Lake Chelan–Sawtooth Wilderness and is more challenging. There are privately owned parcels at various points along the lake-

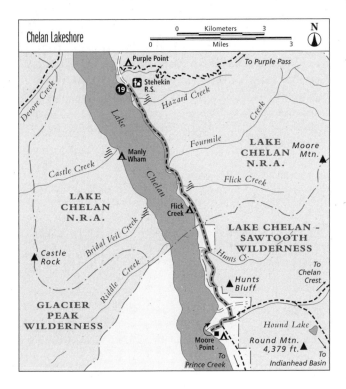

shore, and some have cabins on them. Treat them as private property. Check yourself for ticks after the hike; they are particularly abundant in spring and early summer.

The trail begins as a level trek beside the water, with intermittent views of Castle Rock across the lake. There is a pretty waterfall at Hazard Creek, and just beyond it the trail runs out onto a rocky headland for superb views up and down the lake. Buckner Mountain is the snowy summit far up the Stehekin Valley, and its rocky neighbor is Booker Mountain. In the middle distance, McGregor Mountain presents an immense edifice of rock. The first major stream along the trail is Fourmile Creek, and the trail wanders inland here to cross an alluvial fan. Back on the lakeshore, the trail soon runs eastward into the woods to cross Flick Creek at the mouth of its rocky canyon. A moderate climb then leads to a grassy hilltop for more fine views of Lake Chelan. The Flick Creek camp occupies a sparsely wooded point farther to the south, offering a picnic spot with outstanding views.

After passing the camp, the trail leaves Lake Chelan National Recreation Area and enters the Wenatchee National Forest. The route now runs inland, climbing moderately. A side trip along Hunts Creek leads far to the east, after which the trail climbs onto a stony bluff for superb views of the head of the lake. The view continues to improve as the path charts a high and sometimes cliff-hanging course across the face of Hunts Bluff. To the southwest, magnificent crags rise beyond the settlement of Lucerne in the Glacier Peak Wilderness. Turn around here and retrace the trail to complete the hike.

Miles and Directions

0.0   Trail leaves Stehekin bearing southward along lakeshore.

0.5   Falls on Hazard Creek.

2.3   Trail crosses Fourmile Creek.

2.9   Trail crosses Flick Creek.

3.6   Flick Creek camp.

3.7   Trail leaves Lake Chelan National Recreation Area and enters Lake Chelan–Sawtooth Wilderness.

4.4   Trail crosses Hunts Creek.

5.0   Trail reaches its highest point on Hunts Bluff. Turn around.

10.0   Arrive back at trailhead.

20 Stehekin River Trail

Type of hike: Out-and-back.
Distance: 7.0 miles.
Time required: 3 to 5.5 hours.
Elevation change: Minimal.
Best season: Mid-April to early November.

Maps: USGS Stehekin; Green Trails Stehekin.
Jurisdiction: Lake Chelan National Recreation Area (National Park Service).

Finding the trailhead: Take the shuttle bus from the Golden West Visitor Center to the bridge to Harlequin Campground (about 4.8 miles from the Stehekin landing). Cross the bridge and enter Harlequin Campground. The trail begins at the south end of the campground loop.

The Hike

This trail follows the west side of the Stehekin River to a backcountry campground at the head of Lake Chelan. For the most part, the trail runs through a diverse bottomland forest, but there are periodic views of the Stehekin River and the surrounding mountains. This hike is particularly rewarding in late September, when the hardwoods are turning colors.

From the depths of the old-growth cedars at Harlequin Campground, the trail runs south beside old flood channels in the forest. It soon breaks out into the open at the edge of the Stehekin airstrip; turn left at a junction beyond the clearing. Running southward, the trail climbs over the alluvial fan of Blackberry Creek. The river can be seen from this low rise, and there is a glorious view of Rainbow Falls at the far edge of the valley. The trail then descends back into

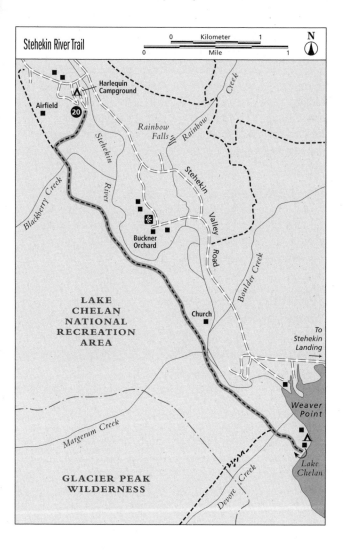

Stehekin River Trail

0   Kilometer   1
0   Mile   1

Airfield

Harlequin
Campground

20

Rainbow
Falls

Rainbow
Creek

Stehekin

Stehekin
River

Blackberry Creek

Buckner
Orchard

Stehekin
Valley
Road

Boulder Creek

LAKE
CHELAN
NATIONAL
RECREATION
AREA

Church

To
Stehekin
Landing

Margerum Creek

Weaver
Point

Lake
Chelan

GLACIER PEAK
WILDERNESS

Devore Creek

the bottoms, where stands of conifers are interspersed with groves of moisture-loving hardwoods. Cottonwood, bigleaf maple, red alder, and aspen are among the more common deciduous trees here, and they provide fall colors in September. There are sporadic views of the Stehekin River as it curves lazily from one side of the valley to the other.

At a well-marked junction, the Devore Creek Trail runs westward into the Glacier Peak Wilderness. Our route runs southward, crossing the alluvial rubble brought down by Devore Creek. After crossing this stream, the path follows an old telephone right-of-way to the shore of Lake Chelan. Here, Weaver Point camp occupies a dense stand of Douglas fir beside the beach. Turn around here and retrace the trail to complete the hike.

Miles and Directions

- **0.0** Harlequin Campground.
- **0.5** Junction beside Stehekin airstrip. Turn left for Weaver Point.
- **0.7** Trail crosses Blackberry Creek.
- **2.3** Trail crosses Margerum Creek.
- **3.2** Junction with Devore Creek Trail. Continue straight ahead.
- **3.3** Trail crosses Devore Creek.
- **3.5** Weaver Point camping area. Turn around.
- **7.0** Arrive back at Harlequin Campground.

21 Rainbow Loop

Type of hike: Shuttle.
Distance: 4.6 miles.
Time required: 2.5 to 5 hours.
Elevation change: 1,050-foot gain.
Best season: Mid-June to mid-October.
Maps: USGS Stehekin; Green Trails Stehekin.
Jurisdiction: Lake Chelan National Recreation Area (National Park Service).

Finding the trailhead: Take the shuttle bus from the Golden West Visitor Center to the upper trailhead, 5 miles above the Stehekin landing and just beyond the bridge to Harlequin Campground. The hike ends at the lower trailhead, 3 miles above the Stehekin landing near the mouth of Boulder Creek, and also on the shuttle bus route.

The Hike

The Rainbow Loop offers a somewhat challenging day trip that climbs onto the middle slopes of the mountains for views of the Stehekin Valley and the peaks that guard it. For visitors who lack the time or inclination to tackle the more challenging trails in the area, the Rainbow Loop offers the best opportunity to view the scenery of the Stehekin Valley. It is easiest when approached from the north. An extra 1-mile climb up the rather steep Rainbow Creek Trail leads to a high viewpoint that looks south across the head of Lake Chelan.

The trail begins by climbing modestly but steadily through a shady forest of Douglas fir. Bigleaf maple occupies the wetter soils, and in early October it bursts into a colorful display of fall foliage. On the way up this section of the trail, talus slopes provide glimpses of the surrounding

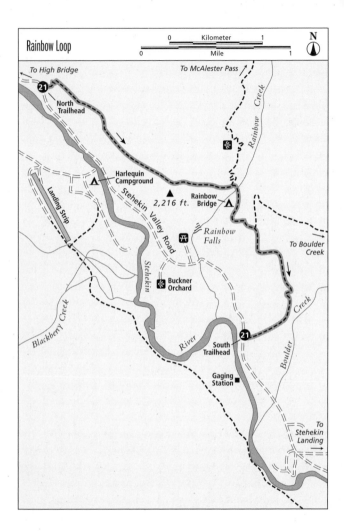

Rainbow Loop

To High Bridge

To McAlester Pass

21 North Trailhead

Rainbow Creek

Harlequin Campground

Stehekin Valley Road

2,216 ft.

Rainbow Bridge

Rainbow Falls

To Boulder Creek

Buckner Orchard

Stehekin

Blackberry Creek

River

Boulder Creek

South Trailhead **21**

Gaging Station

To Stehekin Landing

Landing Strip

N

0 Kilometer 1

0 Mile 1

country. Just after the trail completes its initial climb and begins traversing southward, a bedrock overlook below the trail provides panoramic views of the Stehekin Valley, with the river winding through its forested bottoms. The steep-walled peaks beyond the river are outriders of Sisi Ridge and Tupshin Peak.

After a long, level stretch, the trail begins climbing once more. There is another viewpoint at the edge of a grassy hillside, after which the trail climbs to the top of a timbered platform. Now winding east into the Rainbow Creek drainage, the path crosses a grassy meadow dotted with ponderosa pines. The junction with the Rainbow Creek Trail is at the far edge of this meadow; ambitious visitors can follow it upward for 1 mile to reach a lofty overlook. Otherwise, follow the Rainbow Loop southward as it descends to cross a bridge over Rainbow Creek. There is a shady camping area on the far bank of the stream.

The slopes above the camp are studded with Douglas firs that are dying from heavy infestations of parasitic dwarf mistletoe, often called "witches' broom," which causes the growth of ball-shaped masses of twigs. Tupshin Peak rises dead ahead as the trail surmounts the next finger ridge. Atop the ridge is a rocky clearing that overlooks the Buckner Orchard. McGregor Mountain rises prominently to the north.

After passing a junction with the Boulder Creek Trail, the Rainbow Loop embarks on a steady grade that leads down the mountainside, through stands of Douglas fir and groves of bigleaf maple. It soon arrives at a clifftop perch that faces southward across the head of Lake Chelan. A long and steady descent leads to the mouth of the Boulder Creek valley. Here, the trail turns west to descend the gentle slopes that lead down toward the Stehekin River. The last portion of the trek runs through a sunny woodland to reach a trailhead on the Stehekin Valley Road.

Miles and Directions

0.0 North trailhead.
2.4 Junction with Rainbow Creek Trail. Stay right for loop.
2.6 Trail crosses Rainbow Creek.
2.8 Rainbow Bridge camp.
3.2 Junction with Boulder Pass Trail. Stay right.
4.6 South trailhead.

22 Coon Lake

Type of hike: Out-and-back.
Distance: 2.2 miles.
Time required: 1 to 2 hours.
Elevation change: 610-foot gain.
Best season: Late May to mid-
October.
Maps: Green Trails McGregor Mountain.
Jurisdiction: North Cascades National Park.

Finding the trailhead: Take the shuttle bus from the Golden West Visitor Center to High Bridge. The trail departs from the old High Bridge guard station, behind the buildings.

The Hike

This easy stroll provides rewarding mountain scenery on its way to a marshy lake at the foot of McGregor Mountain.

The trail begins by ascending the wooded benches to the east of High Bridge. The mountain vistas start early on this trail, with good views up Agnes Creek toward the sharp spires of Agnes Mountain. After a short distance, the Coon

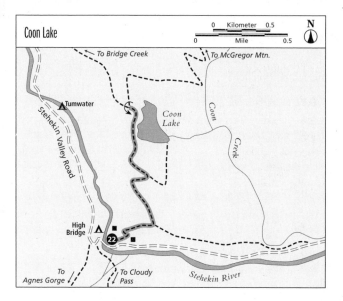

Lake horse trail departs to the right for even better views before reaching a bluff above the south shore of the lake. The main trail climbs northward through the ponderosa pines and Douglas firs to reach the western shore of Coon Lake. This rare mountain wetland is an important staging area for waterfowl. Boggy islands rise in the midst of the water, and the craggy western face of McGregor Mountain soars above the far shore. Retrace your steps to complete the hike.

Miles and Directions

- **0.0** Trailhead at old High Bridge guard station.
- **0.2** Junction with horse trail to Cascade Corrals. Bear left.
- **0.4** Junction with horse trail to south shore of Coon Lake. Bear left.

1.1 Coon Lake. Turn around.

2.2 Arrive back at the trailhead.

23 Agnes Gorge

Type of hike: Out-and-back.
Distance: 5.0 miles.
Time required: 2 to 4 hours.
Elevation change: 430-foot gain.
Best season: Late May to mid-October.

Maps: Green Trails McGregor Mountain; Trails Illustrated North Cascades.
Jurisdiction: North Cascades National Park; Glacier Peak Wilderness (Wenatchee National Forest).

Finding the trailhead: Take the shuttle bus from the Golden West Visitor Center to High Bridge. The trail leaves the Stehekin Valley Road between High Bridge and High Bridge camp. Do not take the Agnes Creek Trail (marked "Pacific Crest Trail"), which is a different trail.

The Hike

This trail makes an excellent short day hike from High Bridge, visiting waterfalls and a narrow gorge on Agnes Creek. The trail begins in the woodlands, providing superb examples of the influence of microclimates on forest communities: The dry, sunny hillsides at the mouth of the Agnes Creek valley are home to drought- and fire-tolerant species such as Douglas fir, ponderosa pine, manzanita, and kinnikinnick. As the trail progresses into moist pockets of shade, red cedar, grand fir, and mountain ash become the dominant trees. As the trail approaches the boundary of the Glacier Peak Wilderness, bigleaf maple becomes prevalent,

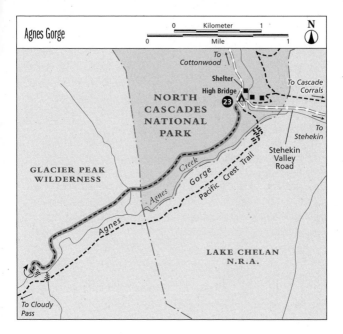

Kilometer

Mile

N

To
Cottonwood

Shelter

High Bridge

23

NORTH
CASCADES
NATIONAL
PARK

To Cascade
Corrals

To
Stehekin

Stehekin
Valley
Road

GLACIER PEAK
WILDERNESS

Creek

Agnes   Gorge

Pacific Crest Trail

Agnes

Agnes

LAKE CHELAN
N.R.A.

To Cloudy
Pass

and along with the aspens just beyond the boundary, they provide superb fall foliage in early October.

The forest soon opens up into a sparse growth of Douglas fir and shrubs, and the jagged spires of Agnes Mountain rise in regal grandeur to the west. The trail now flirts with the edge of the Agnes Gorge for the first time, with the gorge's sheer walls of Skagit gneiss facing the wooded slopes of the near bank. After crossing a pretty woodland stream, the path begins to descend through an old-growth stand of grand fir, Douglas fir, and red cedar. Steep cliffs now line both sides of the gorge, and a spur path leads to an old bridge footing for a humbling clifftop perspective of the chasm. There are no safety restraints here—stay away from the edge! The main trail continues straight ahead, making a brief but rather steep descent to reach the water's edge at the upper end of the gorge. Here, a roaring cataract plunges into a turquoise pool, and hardy conifers grow out of chinks in the rugged cliffs. Turn around here and retrace the trail to complete the hike.

Miles and Directions

0.0 Agnes Gorge Trailhead near High Bridge camp.

1.2 Trail enters the Glacier Peak Wilderness

2.4 Overlook of gorge and waterfalls.

2.5 Trail ends beside Agnes Creek. Turn around.

5.0 Arrive back at trailhead.

About the Author

Erik Molvar has spent decades exploring the wildlands of the West. He has hiked over 10,000 miles of trails, from the Arctic Ocean to the Mexican border. Erik has a master's degree in wildlife management from the University of Alaska Fairbanks, where he performed groundbreaking research on moose in Denali National Park. He currently is the director of Wyoming's Biodiversity Conservation Alliance, one of the most effective conservation groups in the west.

Also by the author:
Hiking the North Cascades
Hiking Olympic National Park
Best Easy Day Hikes: Olympics
Hiking Glacier and Waterton Lakes National Parks
Best Easy Day Hikes: Glacier and Waterton Lakes
Hiking Montana's Bob Marshall Wilderness
Hiking Arizona's Cactus Country
Hiking Zion and Bryce Canyon National Parks
Best Easy Day Hikes: Zion and Bryce
Alaska on Foot: Wilderness Techniques for the Far North
Scenic Driving Alaska and the Yukon
Hiking Wyoming's Cloud Peak Wilderness
Wild Wyoming
Hiking Colorado's Maroon Bells–Snowmass Wilderness

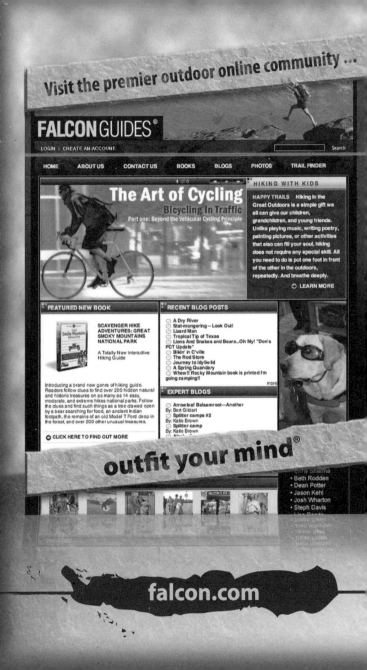